Wisdom Words for Teen Girls 13-18

Practical Activities for Self-Doubt and Stress-Management, Regain Resilience and Mental Health with Mindfulness

By

Stevie Wilcox

Sellix Publications

About the Author

Stevie Wilcox is the person to turn to for reliable techniques, healthcare treatments, and literature suggestions encouraging the proper development and growth of young people, teenage girls, and adults alike. She has kids of her own, so she knows how important it is to give them a good start in life, and she wants to help other parents do the same. Stevie Wilcox devotes a great deal of time and energy to helping kids of all ages. She helps students gain the self-assurance they need to succeed as speakers and managers by engaging them in tasks that reduce their anxiety.

Author's Goal: To answer reader questions and provide proof for claims stated in the introduction. Her treatment, psychological techniques, and activities are quite effective, making her stand out from the rest.

Contents

Words of Advice

Don't be bothered by how other people see or make you feel. People will perceive you in a positive light if they choose to. Nothing you can do will change the minds of those who are set on seeing you as an evil individual. The more effort you put into convincing them of your sincerity, the more weapons you offer them to use against you. Maintain a positive attitude and trust in your abilities. ***Have faith in what you're doing and maintain your focus forward rather than on those who would bring you down.*** Simply put, you can't make others see things your way. It would be best if you trust that you have the power to make positive changes in your life and that no one else can do it for you.

We are destined to blunder along the way. We were born with inherent weaknesses. And I do mean all of us. We may all be liars at times. There are moments when we all give in to desires. It's human nature to pass judgment and offer empty promises. ***The fact that we each make errors in our unique ways does not minimize the significance of learning from them and improving in the future.*** If you think the world can change, you must be willing to alter your behavior. So go ahead. Start.

Introduction

Have you ever been in one of those situations where you keep scrolling an Instagram model's feed and comparing yourself to her? Have you ever doubted yourself before even starting a task? There must be times when you feel that you will only be able to complete your tasks after the deadline and will eventually fail. You have the feeling that nothing will ever go in your way. You do not live in the moment and are always worried about the future or constantly thinking about your past mistakes.

Do not worry!

Wisdom Workbook for Teen Girls 13-18 is here to solve your problems.

This book contains the information you need to identify your insecurities and self-doubts. It also provides you with tips and strategies for overcoming your insecurities and start trusting in your abilities. It emphasizes the importance of having positive and healthy self-confidence in one's self and allows you to recognize the different types of insecurities that teenage girls have nowadays.

This book also provides you with complete knowledge about the effects of stress on your personal and academic life. *It explains the reactions that are carried out in our bodies when we are stressed and also gives details about the main reasons for stress in teenage girls.* It also gives you exciting strategies and ways to minimize your stressors, helps you schedule your tasks, maintain a healthy diet, have a positive morning ritual and much more!

This book has a complete guideline that focuses on the meaning of mindfulness. *It expresses the significance of mindfulness in a teenager's life and how one can start practicing mindfulness even at home.* It contains a wide range of exercises and strategies that teenage girls can practice regularly to start living in the moment and not worrying about the future or their past mistakes.

It gives you details on the link between resilience and mindfulness. It also expresses the importance of resilience and its benefits. *It contains a variety of mindful strategies and tips on training teenage girls to become resilient.* From initiating mantras to practicing different mindful exercises, this book contains everything regarding gaining resilience through mindfulness.

Along with this, the Wisdom Workbook for Teen Girls aged 13-18 also focuses on having positive mental health and the benefits of having good mental health. *It also explains in detail the relationship between positive mental health and mindfulness.* It provides you with mindful strategies to overcome your negative emotions and thoughts and have positive mental health.

Chapter 1: It is never too Late to Fall in Love with Yourself

It is time to start your healing journey and become the best version of yourself. No one understands you better than yourself. So stop doubting and start trusting yourself more!

1.1: Never Let Your Doubts Define You

There are times when you see your class fellows receiving a prize or becoming the president of any club. And you think to yourself, **"She is so smart; I will never be able to be as smart as her."** Or you may find yourself wishing and saying, **"If only God would have blessed me with such intelligence."**

Do not worry! Let's take our first step in clearing all doubts and insecurities we have built up inside our minds throughout our lives. Let's start with gaining a complete understanding of the doubts we have about ourselves.

What is Self-Doubt?

No one is entirely pleased with every aspect of themselves, not even the most confident and loud women. *We all experience moments of self-doubt, whether over a decision we made, a word we spoke, or a desire to become a better version of ourselves.*

When it comes to our bodies, careers, intelligence, ages, and relationships, we women don't always feel completely confident. Whether it's the first day at a new school, a big test, or a big game, we all have moments of uncertainty in our abilities. That's the way it usually is.

The term "self-doubt" describes people's doubts about themselves, their abilities, or their choices. Because of internalizing these damaging doubts, we start to believe that we are not good enough.

Self-doubt is the inability to believe in one's strengths and potential. It's a way of thinking that prevents you from achieving your goals and having faith in yourself. While it's admirable to be humble, it's counterproductive to put yourself last to please others. Our fears and apprehensions prevent us from achieving the good that we are capable of if we only try. This implies that when we have doubts, we tend to give up.

It's easy to become obsessed with today's social media and platforms like Instagram, where we constantly compare ourselves to others and feel immense pressure and stress to achieve "perfection" despite knowing that there is nothing like perfection. As a result, we may feel unworthy and insecure, which can lower our self-esteem and make us feel less confident.

Even if a woman may seem confident and bold on the outside, you never know what battles she will be fighting inside her mind.

Here is a description of what it might feel like in the head of a successful woman who tries to hide and fight her self-doubt and insecurities.

Alicia manages a division that generates millions of dollars annually for a corporation with thousands of workers. She has a history of achievement in executive roles at prominent organizations and a graduate degree. She exudes self-assurance, inspires other women, and values her family above all else. As far as outsiders are concerned, Alicia personifies the ideal of "having it all," and she makes doing so appear effortless.

But the scenario that's running through her mind is very different. She frequently attends executive meetings at work with butterflies in her stomach because she is unsure if her statements are being received positively. Alicia continuously criticizes herself for her perceived lack of expertise on the subject at hand. Despite the praise she receives following important speeches, she is a nervous mess beforehand. In many situations, she freezes up out of fear of being judged as someone stupid.

Alicia feels like a failure as a mother since she doesn't always make supper or volunteer at her children's schools, and she constantly compares herself to other mothers. Regarding her self-image, she frequently finds fault with what she sees when she examines her reflection. She presents herself as confident and booming in public but struggles with insecurity, guilt, self-criticism, and comparison in private.

This is the strength of a woman. This is how a woman represents herself, although when breaking from the inside.

Teenage is a time of pervasive insecurity, and learning to overcome these feelings is a crucial component of becoming an adult. Every teenager deals with anxieties, yet these issues develop differently and to differing degrees for each teen. There are various obstacles to overcome during adolescence. Life is undergoing significant transformation; along with it comes stress, anxiety, doubt, and dread. Under these conditions, even a minor stressor can snowball into considerable anxiety, which might lead to a harmful coping style.

Different Types of Self-Doubts and Insecurities

Teenage girls are subject to pressure from many sources, even inside themselves. Hormonal shifts and pressure from peers, parents, and society can feel like a sword cutting a teen. Teenage is a time when girls begin to make their own choices, explore their identities, and compare themselves to their peers.

Here is a list of self-doubts that teenage girls have nowadays.

• Beauty and Body's Image

Lack of confidence in one's physical appearance is a worldwide problem. Since the 1960s, an increasing number of women—especially young women—have been preoccupied with their appearance. **Girls will do just about everything to get their ideal body image.** Media commercials and movies are to blame for these kinds of body image issues. Having a Barbie or zero-size figure is a dream for teenage girls. Body shaming can also result in teenage girls becoming more aware of their bodies, making them unable to breathe in their own skin.

Most young women nowadays are unhappy with their bodies because of the media's emphasis on thinness and the unrealistic standards it sets for beauty. Teenage anxieties, if left untreated, may follow a person into adulthood. Insecurities run rampant during adolescence and learning to overcome them is crucial to developing into an adult.

• Social Insecurity

Teenage girls are concerned about fitting in socially, fearing the unknown, or being put in uncomfortable circumstances. It can be daunting for teenagers to confront people and places they don't know, whether relocating to a new area, starting a new school, joining a sports team, or even just approaching a different social group. Fear of rejection or ridicule from peers is a form of social insecurity. Adolescents strongly seek out and participate in social situations that involve peer pressure.

• Relationships

Many women have trouble with self-confidence and the feeling that they are desirable in relationships. If you're a woman who often struggles with feelings of rejection and inadequacy, you may compare yourself unfavorably to other women you believe to have it better than you do. **Our natural inclination is to look at what we don't have rather than what we do. We also seek a partner's acceptance and affirmation rather than examining our insecurities and working to improve them.** If you're experiencing relationship insecurity, you lack confidence in your connection. Feeling worried is a symptom of a limiting belief, such as the idea that you aren't good enough for your relationship or don't deserve love. You may have poor self-esteem and struggle with doubting your worth.

You can even live in constant anxiety, wondering what your lover is up to whenever they aren't by your side.

• Intellectual Insecurity

This doubt stems from an awareness that one's intelligence and skills are inadequate. People with this insecurity generally have low self-esteem and believe they are unintelligent. **My observations have led me to the conclusion that many women harbor severe doubts about their abilities to contribute meaningfully to intellectual discussions.**

They worry that they have nothing worth to offer, which is ridiculous. It's not just romantic partners who might trigger feelings of inadequacy; friends, family, and coworkers can do the same.

There are many causes of female insecurity and several strategies for overcoming it. Remember that everyone struggles with something, no matter how secure you feel.

- ## Work Insecurity

Many teenage girls work to support themselves. When women are concerned that they may lose their job, it can cause them to feel insecure and unmotivated. **Persistent anxiety over one's employment status might impact either briefly, during layoffs, terminations, or permanently**. The fear of losing one's job is what's meant by the term "job insecurity."

It's the polar opposite of job security, which is feeling safe in your current position. Whether a layoff is imminent, worrying about your future in the workforce can have severe consequences for your mental and physical health.

Identifying your Insecurities and Self-doubts

Certain types of insecurities are more evident than others. Most people who try to hide their fears do so because they fear being judged negatively, yet avoiding uncomfortable situations makes matters worse. Some of the symptoms of insecurity remain the same over time, while others come and go with little to no notice, and they often overlap with those of low self-esteem and value.

Symptoms of Having Self-Doubts

You can look for these symptoms in yourself if you want to identify your insecurities and self-doubts.

1. You start wearing clothes that are too big for you

You may be self-conscious of your appearance and assume you are fat or not so thin. You might also fear people judging you or making fun of you. As a result, you start wearing baggy clothes because you think that they would hide your body.

2. You have discontinued your social activities.

You might suffer from social insecurity if you have stopped meeting your friends and suddenly started avoiding them. You harshly judge yourself and think you are not good enough to hang out with your peers.

3. You have started talking badly about yourself.

You might have heard yourself saying, "I am not good enough to do this" or "No one ever needs me anyway." You need more self-assurance and confidence. You do not trust your abilities and skills and think that others are better than you.

4. You keep your opinions to yourself.

You do not speak your mind or express your thoughts because you feel unimportant and do not matter. When all your friends decide where to eat or which movie to watch, you keep quiet and let them decide.

1.2 You Know Yourself Better Than Anyone Else

Overthinking your flaws and imperfections destroys all the beauty around you. So, do not let the negative thoughts control you and believe the lies they tell you.

Why do you feel insecure and doubt yourself?

Following are some possible reasons for feeling insecure about yourself. Reading about them would shed light on the symptoms that hold you back.

- *Past Efforts and Failed Attempts*

Your current mood and behavior are probably heavily influenced by your past experiences. **Who you are and how you understand the world are both products of your past experiences.** Many of us struggle to let go of something, and our history of setbacks and letdowns might shake our confidence and courage.

This is especially true if you have had hardships in life, such as an abusive upbringing or an unfair termination from your school.

If you don't take steps to improve your mental health, traumatic events will continue to have a detrimental effect. If you let the mistakes of the past shape your present and future, you will never amount to anything.

- *How you were raised*

Your upbringing is a significant factor in shaping your character and habits as an adult. Imagine you were raised in a household where you were disciplined when you made a mistake or went to a school emphasizing getting good grades. If so, you may have trained yourself to second-guess your abilities constantly.

If you had a rough childhood due to factors like poor parenting, you could be more cautious as an adult. You could be worried about making the same mistakes as your parents. In contrast, if you grow up with parents who are self-centered and vain, you can adopt their attitude. If those traits run in the family, you may take on their modesty or lack of confidence.

You could second-guess yourself just before doing an important task assigned to you. You need help accepting praise from others or realizing when you've excelled at something.

- ## *Comparing yourself with your friends*

Since we are living in a very competitive society, we naturally compare ourselves to others. Maybe some of your friends like bragging about how rich and fabulous they are on social media platforms like Instagram.

By constantly comparing ourselves to others, we set ourselves up to envy their supposedly "perfect" lives and successes. Similarly, we can worry that our performance is lagging behind our peers. When you constantly evaluate yourself about others, you risk losing sight of who you are. You'll be wasting your time worrying about how others live when you can concentrate on improving your life.

- ## *New Difficulties*

It's normal to be unsure about how to go when first faced with a difficult situation. **You may not know what to do because this is the first time you have encountered this situation, and you have no idea what to do next to fix the problem.** As a result of your worry and uncertainty, you may have feelings of insecurity and doubts about your skills.

- ## *Fear of Failing or Fear of Succeeding*

You may have faced a situation where your loved one was envious of your success, resulting in a huge fight. **The worry of making a mistake or failing is just as genuine as the anxiety of being unable to repeat our past successes due to some sad results linked to it.** If you're having difficulty believing in yourself, you could attribute your success to good fortune rather than hard work. You might let your fear of success or failure keep you from reaching your full potential.

Effects of Self-doubts in Your Personal Life

When you doubt yourself, explain your situation by pointing to your feelings.

You train yourself to find reasons why the opportunity is unsuitable. *Consequently, you'll be unable to take advantage of several chances that may help you advance in your career or get closer to realizing your goals.*

Constant and intrusive self-doubt fills you with irrational terror. You can be scared to try new things because you worry about what might happen if you fail. You rarely step outside your safety zone because of your most significant worry, and you can't make the life-or-death choice you know you need to.

Being a woman with more of an emotional mindset than a logical one, you're afraid to love other people. You worry they won't like you or because you worry you don't have what it takes to love someone truly. You're too worried about money to be generous.

You keep your thoughts and feelings to yourself because you're frightened of being misunderstood or coming off as foolish if others find out.

Fear and insecurity are the offspring of doubt. When other people push your buttons or harm your feelings, you will experience these emotions. The effects include an increase in anxiety, paranoia, and a heightened sense of suspicion.

Effects of Self-doubts in Your Academic Life

Despite the effects that self-doubts and insecurities may cause in your personal life, there are several effects that these doubts have on your academic life too.

A few of them are mentioned below.

- *Adjectives like "I'm dumb," "I cannot accomplish this," "I consistently get everything incorrect," "Nobody else loves me," etc. may pop into your head. You may suffer from depression and overthinking.*

- *When faced with challenges, you may choose to give up, avoid taking chances, withdraw from activities, or even switch off your webcams during online classes.*

- *Sometimes, you will excel, but then you will abruptly struggle. You may get high scores in a subject and then suddenly get low scores in the same subject after some time.*

- *To feel more in control of your life and overcome your low self-esteem, you may exert authority over the actions of your other class fellows.*

- *You may need help dealing with frustration or hesitate to attempt anything new. You may also log out of the virtual learning environment unexpectedly, act aggressively, like a prankster, or pretend to be ignorant.*

- *You might worry that people have unrealistically high expectations from you because of your recent accomplishment.*

1.3: It is Time to Write a New Story

No matter if you're starting a new career, becoming a blogger, taking an exam, or competing in a sport, you'll inevitably have moments of self-doubt. But if you let those doubts fester for too long, they can begin to manifest in your body as well as your mind.

If you are a girl who is struggling with self-doubt and insecurity, here are several approaches that may assist.

1. Accept your differences

According to a powerful adage, comparing steals your happiness. In many contexts, this proverb proves true. When women question themselves because they are worried they won't be as successful as someone else, they may find it difficult to go forward. *Each person has their unique path and definition of success. Regardless of other people's circumstances or actions, all we can truly control and concentrate on is our journey and the direction we choose to take it.*

If you want to achieve calmness and become a fearless woman, you need to accept the things you can't change about yourself, such as your nose, eyes or family. You may even like your differences if you can learn to celebrate your uniqueness. Accepting the parts about yourself that are challenging might help you grow.

2. Practice Self-compassion and self-kindness

If someone you care about makes a mistake, you might forgive them. But you might beat yourself up or talk negatively about yourself when you do something wrong. You will never be able to relinquish the guilt of making that error again. This is all because you fail to treat yourself with self-compassion and self-kindness.

Practicing self-kindness is treating oneself with compassion and understanding in situations where one has experienced disappointment or suffering. When we are already in pain, rather than being critical of ourselves or condemning ourselves harshly, we may treat ourselves with warmth and kindness.

Here are a few ways you can practice self-compassion when having hard days.

- *Take a hot shower or bath and let yourself rest*

- *Catch up or call an old friend*

- *Go on a walk alone and observe your surroundings*

- *Read your favorite book or eat your favorite food*

3. Put your negative thoughts to test

Thinking negatively may be highly detrimental to our health. When these thoughts continue to build upon one another, they frequently result in feelings of anxiety or depression. We need to have the necessary skills to effectively sort out unproductive thinking. This has the potential to assist us in leading happier, more fulfilling lives.

One of the most effective ways to combat negative thinking is to recognize your negative thinking pattern. Once you have recognized your negative thinking pattern, you can control your emotions and thoughts.

Here are some types of negative thinking patterns.

Black-and-white thinking

In such thinking, you see things from two perspectives and cannot comprehend any other perspective or result.

Personalizing

In this type of thinking, you take all of the blame on yourself and do not criticize anyone else for the mistake.

Filter Thinking

In this type of thinking, you see things from only a negative perspective and assume all the adverse outcomes.

Journaling

Journaling is a type of self-expression that stimulates feelings, which in turn improves mental health, facilitates self-discovery, and aids in understanding and expressing emotions. It can facilitate communication with the unconscious and the recognition of unhelpful ideas, paving the way for the adoption of more constructive mental habits.

Writing in a journal might help you overcome feelings of worthlessness, and spending even just a few minutes writing down your thoughts helps you to start seeing and understanding your ideas.

Here are a few journal prompts that may enhance your self-esteem, help you overcome your insecurities, and become a strong and self-assured girl.

PRACTISING SELF-LOVE PROMPTS

What are the situations that make you feel the most peaceful? What are the ways through which you can experience these situations more often?

What is the one way that can help you fall in love with yourself more?

List down 7 things that make you feel loveable.

Visualize the person that you wish to be in 5 years. Explain her in detail. Write down all the things that she loves, her habits, her job and everything that you could think of.

Express your feelings about a difficult situation that you fought. Also, explain the strategies and ways in which you overcame that situation.

Express gratitude to your body by writing a letter to yourself.

If you did not care about the opinion of others, in what ways would you be enjoying your life?

List down 3 insecurities and how you think you can overcome them.

List down 15 things that tend to inspire you.

a). Self-Affirmations and Positive Self Talk

Affirmations for self-esteem are positive self-talk consisting of remarks, phrases, or sentences that may be repeated to reinforce optimistic beliefs and emotions. If you are a woman with low self-esteem or low confidence and searching for a confidence boost, these exercises can be a lifesaver.

The purpose of positive affirmations is to assist people stop engaging in destructive internal dialogue. You choose to be nice to yourself and others, to dwell on the positive, and to have an even stronger belief in yourself. Reward yourself and boost your confidence whenever you do anything significant at work. Here are a few things that you can do to boost your self-esteem and overcome your insecurities and self-doubts.

- *Maintain a desktop or mobile app where you save compliments received.*

- *Writing your achievements for yourself to read over when you're feeling low is a great confidence booster.*

- *Practice self-love by taking a few moments every day to write down three things you like about yourself.*

Self-affirmations for daily practice

- I have faith in myself.

- I am an independent and complete woman.

- I am beautiful just the way I am.

- I am sufficient for myself.

- I decide to always cherish myself.

- I love myself and the person I am becoming.

- I deserve all the happiness in the world.

- I am blessed and grateful to have a healthy body, a blessed life and my unique abilities.

- I can handle all the obstacles in the way of my goals.

- I decide to look at the world through love and compassion.

- I can accomplish all of my goals.

- I can stand up for the truth.

- I can protect myself and my loved ones.

- I say "Yes" to all the positive things coming my way.

- I am loved, accepted and appreciated just the way I am.

b. Enlisting your past achievements

There will be times when you are feeling less than confident, and your friends or older sister will come to soothe you. She begins by listing all of your accomplishments, and you begin to feel better.

But what will you do if you are alone and your insecurities start hitting you?

Do not worry! Here is a simple tip to overcome self-doubt and insecurities within a few minutes.

Take a clean sheet of paper and start writing a letter to yourself. Remind yourself of all of your achievements and start listing them individually. **Write down the compliments and appreciation that you achieved on your achievements.** Ultimately, start reading your letter to yourself and watch your insecurities disappear!

The Flower Exercise

This is a mindful exercise that you can do to understand your differences and uniqueness better. Carry out this activity whenever you feel like comparing yourself with another person.

- *Pick three different flowers.*

- *Close your eyes and enter a state of deep relaxation by gently stroking the petals of a flower while you count them off one by one. Check out the size, shape, and texture variations.*

- *With eyes wide open, spend two minutes carefully studying each blossom. Now, take a close look at the petals of each flower, noting their hue and smoothness.*

- *Next, focus on the aromas of each flower and see if you can identify and differentiate them.*

- *Now take a sheet of paper and write down how each flower was different from the other and was unique and beautiful.*

Choosing your friend circle wisely

One of the worst things for our mental health is spending time with people who constantly put us down. *You might have experienced such times when your friends would not appreciate your good grades and would be jealous of them. Or there might be a time when you would have gotten a new haircut, and nobody appreciated it in your friend group.* Spend time with those who lift your spirits and appreciate you. They'll be a source of encouragement even when you can't muster any for yourself. The best way to boost your self-esteem and feel accepted for who you are is to surround yourself with positive, encouraging individuals.

Visualize your best self

Ladies, we need to ask ourselves a crucial question: are we the women we see ourselves to be? Do we regularly begin our days feeling strong and capable, ready to take on the world? If the answer is affirmative, then you should be praised. But if you have doubts about who you are, it's time to go for that idealized version of yourself.

Let me be quite clear: your appearance is irrelevant to me. I want you to be outstanding in all parts of your life, not just your physical appearance. A few years ago, I was exactly where you are now. Fearful and insecure, I felt insignificant in the face of the vastness and disorder of the world. Although I had grown weary of my negative status, it was time to become positive. I sought joy, positive emotion, and vitality. I started nourishing my mind by reading various books on spirituality and personal growth because you are what you eat, so the saying goes.

Here are simple tips on how to visualize your best self.

• Choose Your Goals

Where do you want to put your attention? Start by focusing on a single aspiration or objective. For instance, if you have a presentation coming up next week, try picturing it going well.

• Envision the Scene

Imagine the setting in great detail. Avoid confusion by visualizing vivid scenes and events; this will enhance the effectiveness of your vision.

When practicing visualization, drawing upon all of your senses is essential. Incorporate all senses — sight, sound, taste, smell, and touch — to fully realize your objective. For instance, in the example of giving a presentation, picture yourself as the head of the group. Think of the group members' faces and their clothes. Feel the sun's warmth streaming through the windows as you listen to the rustle of papers and the aroma of freshly brewed coffee.

Think about how you feel and what it is like for you. You feel ready and enthusiastic about giving your presentation. You're confident that your coworkers will appreciate what you say and learn from your input. You're eager to get going right now.

• Visualize Your Way to a Prosperous Outcome

Start thinking about the steps you will need to take to guarantee the success of your presentation. Figure out what needs to happen for you to succeed. And as part of your visualization exercise, start imagining yourself carrying out each action. The introduction is the first section of your presentation. So, picture yourself briefing the audience on the presentation's purpose and the takeaways.

• Daily Visualization

If your presentation is in two weeks, visualize it in full at least once a day leading up to the big day. Maintaining a regular visualization practice is crucial because it trains your brain to accept the imagined reality as accurate.

Let's Solve These Worksheets Together

Here are a few worksheets to help you make peace with your insecurities and boost your confidence and self-esteem.

Enhancing My Self-Esteem

Traits that make me feel proud

_____

_____

_____

_____

4 Compliments that I received made me feel beautiful

_____

_____

_____

_____

Name of my loved ones who feel blessed to have me in their life

_____

_____

_____

_____

My Compliment Jar

Write down all the kind things people have said to you and put them in this jar.

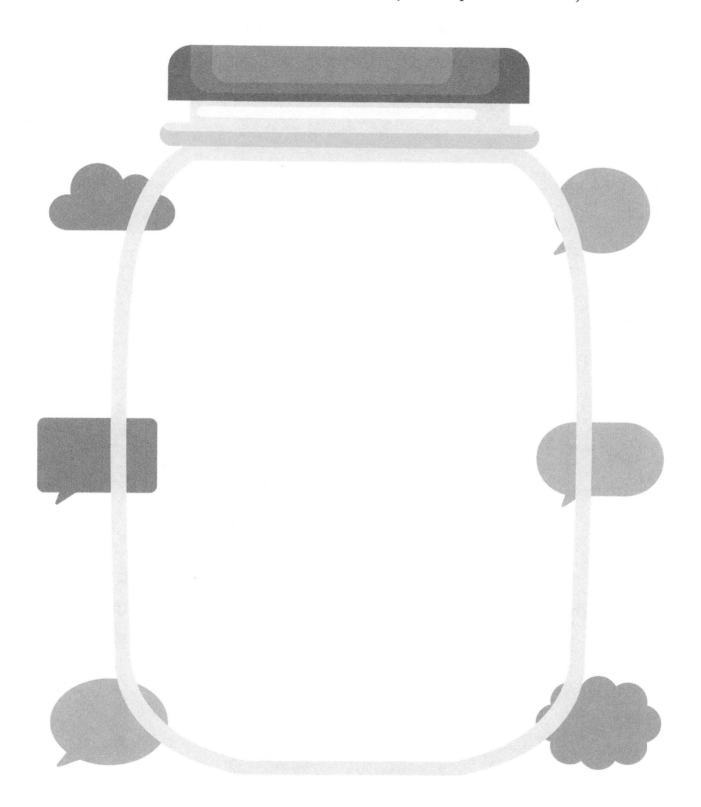

Reflecting on yourself

1- What are the things that make you fall in love with yourself?

2- What are the things that keep you happy?

3- As you glance yourself in the mirror, what do you see?

4- What are the things that you learnt about yourself in this week?

Learning More about Who I am

Answer the inquiries below. There are no rules and regulations. Write whatever is in your heart and mind!

Am I content and pleased with who I am right now? Explain why or why not?

_____

_____

_____

_____

_____

_____

_____

How would I describe my greater self? Explain.

_____

_____

_____

_____

_____

_____

_____

_____

Monthly Self-Reflection

The accomplishments that make me feel proud

_____

_____

_____

Lessons I have learnt this month

_____

_____

_____

Things that need work on my part

_____

_____

_____

Efforts that others can do to support me

_____

_____

_____

Some Powerful Tips for My Girls!

Take some time from your busy schedule and reflect on the positive and good things in your life. Be proud of how far you have come and become excited about how much more you have to achieve. This life offers you thousands of opportunities that you can take only if you believe in yourself enough. Here are a few tips for practicing to become the best version of yourself.

- *Always maintain eye contact while having a conversation with someone.*

- *Always enter a room with a good posture and a confident mindset.*

- *Choose your signature scent.*

- *Always compliment others.*

- *Be open to experiencing new things.*

- *Recognize the beauty that the earth brings.*

- *Never hold your laugh back!*

Chapter 2: It All Begins and Ends in Your Mind

The power to select positive thoughts over negative ones is the most potent tool in the fight against stress.

2.1: A Day Goes Well Before Stress Comes Along

One of the most fascinating, exciting, and challenging times in practically anyone's life is their teenage years. When we're in our teens, life gets fascinating and intense because many people are trying to figure out who they are and where they fit in. Teenagers are increasingly confronted with issues in their everyday lives, both at home and school and in their interpersonal connections. Teenage may be difficult since it requires the development of new behavioral models, adapting to social standards, and pursuing one's position in society.

What is stress?

When we feel threatened or under duress, our bodies and minds react to stress. This is common when we feel helpless or powerless over situations. Stress is a part of life for everyone. "Stress" refers to an unpleasant mental state in which one feels pressured. School, employment, extracurricular, friends, and family are major contributors to adolescent stress.

Positive stress may spur females to accomplish great things, but negative stress's unpleasant and damaging effects can manifest in various ways. It's more challenging to adjust and deal with when stress is constant or overwhelming. Some women develop a tolerance for stress because of its constant presence in their lives. Often, women are too busy to stop and consider the adverse effects of stress on their lives.

Teenage girls experience potentially stressful events daily, which may intensify as they reach adulthood. It's essential to learn to manage stress so that they may have a fulfilling life while still being productive at school.

When under stress, the body goes through a specific physiological process. An "adrenaline rush" occurs when adrenaline interacts with another hormone called epinephrine. The hormones and substances trigger a rise in cardiovascular output and blood pressure. These processes help the body prepare for and recover from a threat. When the body needs to ramp up its defensive mechanisms, it reduces the production of certain chemicals. Chronic stress can develop in the brain if it is always alert. Whether the event is real or imagined, the same effects occur. High blood pressure, acid reflux, asthma, ulcers, and migraines are among possible side effects.

Teenagers' lives can be negatively impacted by the cumulative effects of daily stress that can last far into adulthood. All signs of stress disappear once the brain realizes there is no danger. Unfortunately, some people fail to recognize that the threat has passed, which can lead to disastrous consequences. Most teenage girls experience stress and need to master stress management skills to thrive in today's complex and demanding environment.

Anxiety, sadness, and hopelessness can arise when stress builds up without release or conservative treatment. The prevalence of mental illness among teenage girls is rising, and a major contributing factor is the pressures young girls feel to perform well in school.

High school students' performance in life can be negatively impacted by the amount of pressure they experience, and first-hand experiences can shed a lot of light on the realities of kids' daily struggles.

Different things that girls stress about

Here are a few different stressors that may trigger stress and anxiety in teenage women.

- ## Study Pressure

Teens have much to worry about regarding school, from grades and tests to college applications. Adolescents commonly have concerns about school, impressing adults, and keeping up with peers. Academic stress can also result from a lack of time management skills or a general sense of being swamped by schoolwork.

- ## Social Pressures

Teenage girls put a premium on hanging out with their friends. Since they spend so much time with their peers, it can be difficult for them to separate from them.

Teens are under much pressure and struggle to learn to handle healthy disagreements and navigate their relationships. At the same time as they face the everyday stresses of growing up, girls must also deal with the pressures of their peers. They will sometimes act in ways that are outside their comfort zones in an attempt to make and keep up with their friends.

- ## Disagreement within the Family

Any source of strain in the home will likely affect teenage girls the most. An increase in women's stress can result from many different factors, including unrealistic expectations from parents, poor sibling relationships (including sibling bullying), illness in the family, and financial hardships in the family.

- ## Stressful Events around the Globe

The stress caused by school shootings, terrorist attacks, and natural catastrophes isn't just felt by adults. Teens are exposed to the news around the clock, and hearing frightening reports from their own country and worldwide can make them fear for their personal and family security.

- ## Major Shifts in life

Stress is a normal part of life at any age, and teenage girls are no exception. Teens might get overwhelmed by life events like relocating, beginning high school, or experiencing a divorce or split family. Not understanding how to deal with significant change may be terrifying and perplexing for a maturing woman.

2.2: A Diamond is Just a Charcoal That Handled Stress Well

One of the best ways to find calm within is to train your brain to ignore distractions. The path to contentment and fulfillment lies in prioritizing your sense of calm over your desire to be always correct.

Symptoms of Stress

There are several ways in which stress may modify how we feel, act, and how our bodies function. When we're under pressure, it might be easy to see it immediately. On other occasions, however, we may choose to ignore the warnings and carry on with our work regardless.

Feelings, actions, thoughts, and even physical health can all be negatively impacted by stress. However, because people have different coping mechanisms, stress symptoms can range. Symptoms may be difficult to pinpoint and overlap with those of other illnesses.

Here are a few symptoms you may experience if you suffer from stress.

- *Emotional Symptoms*

- *These are some of the emotional signs of stress:*

- *Turning irritable*

- *anger issues*

- *Becoming moody*

- *Feeling like you need to take charge or that you are losing control*

- *Struggling to unwind and calm your thoughts*

- *Having a negative opinion of oneself (poor self-esteem)*

- *Feelings of isolation, low self-esteem, and low confidence.*

- *Keeping away from other people.*

Physical Symptoms of Stress

Some of the physical manifestations of stress are:

- *Low Energy*

- *Headaches*

- *Nausea, vomiting, and gastrointestinal distress such as diarrhea or constipation*

- *Soreness, stiffness, and muscular tension*

- *Aching chest and a racing heart*

- *Insomnia*

- *Continual illness from colds and flu*

- *Lack of sexual interest*

- *Extreme Palpitations, trembling body, a buzzing in the ears, and cold or sweaty hands and feet*

- *Problems swallowing and dry mouth*

- *Tense muscles in the mouth and clenched teeth*

Cognitive Symptoms of Stress

Some of the mental manifestations of stress are:

- *Persistent anxiety*

- *Fast-paced thinking*

- *Lack of focus and disarray*

- *Lack of concentration*

- *Poor discretion*

- *Adopting a negative outlook or attitude*

Behavioral Changes from Stress

Examples of stress-related changes in behavior are as follows:

- *Alterations in appetite include a lack of hunger or an excess of hunger*

- *Putting off or evading one's duties*

- *Increased consumption of nicotine, alcohol, or narcotics*

- *Showing increased instances of anxiety-inducing actions, including biting nails, fidgeting, and pacing*

Effects of Stress on Your Personal Life

Every girl goes through difficult times now and again. There's not much to worry about if you can settle down afterwards. However, your body will eventually rebel against chronic stress and a lack of rest.

You have discomforts such as aches and pains in your muscles and joints and trouble sleeping. Getting out of bed makes you irritated and exhausted. Feelings of melancholy or sadness may also arise. Because interacting with others drains your energy, you may start acting cruelly toward them and even withdraw from them. It's harder to focus and puts more significant strain on your workload. There are moments when it seems like things will never get better, and life doesn't seem worth living any longer. Everyone reacts differently under pressure. Stress is more likely to affect you if you don't desire to perform things in a good manner while paying less attention to what is going well.

If you take on more work than you can reasonably do, your productivity will suffer. Stressed workers who put in long hours typically accomplish less in that time. It might also cause you to feel down and anxious.

Happy girls live 4-10 years longer than stressful girls (with less harmful and more positive feelings and optimism). Not only do happy girls live longer, but they do so in better health. Positive emotion expressers, such as happy, joyful, and enthusiastic, had a 22% lower risk of developing heart disease. An optimistic outlook was associated with a 30% lower risk of death from coronary heart disease in a study of over 100,000 women. Positive emotions, even daily, are associated with a longer life.

Relationships may suffer from stress, which is unfortunately very common nowadays. The close ones of girls suffering from stress have a hard time understanding what they're going through and supporting them when they bottle up or hide their stress.

Effects of Stress on Your Academic Life

Like other students in higher education, you probably feel the pressure of your studies. It's sometimes okay to be stressed. Stress, in moderate doses, is helpful since it serves as an incentive to keep you focused on your academic goals and prevents you from slacking off.

Even in the "positive stress" zone, your body still expends energy as you try to keep from crossing into the "negative stress" zone. Focus and productivity suffer when stress, worry, and anxiety become overwhelming. Detrimental stress interferes with brain function and has physical consequences, including increased appetite, headaches, and exhaustion. A person's immune system weakens, and they become more prone to catching a cold or becoming sick. It can also have a significant negative impact on the classroom. Finding techniques to relax the mind and body after exposure to stressful events is also crucial.

Prolonged stress can cause increases in cortisol, which can be harmful to the brain in the long run. Researchers have hypothesized that chronic exposure to elevated cortisol levels has a significant role in developing Alzheimer's disease and other kinds of dementia.

Distractions at work make concentrating difficult, increasing worry over our lack of productivity. Most of us don't realize we're losing concentration until we're already over our heads. Focus, concentration, and memory all suffer when mental and emotional tiredness set in. And all of this eventually affects the academic performance of a school teenager.

2.3: Here's to New Beginnings

Remember that most of the stress you experience results from your own reactions and not external events. Just by shifting your mindset, you can eliminate that added stress.

Here is a list of strategies to cope with stress and live a peaceful and healthy life.

Breathing Techniques

With this simple breathing method, you can relieve tension, anxiety, and panic in only a few minutes and without any special equipment.

The best results will come from making it a consistent part of your everyday life. It may be done in various positions, including standing, sitting in a chair with back support, sitting on a yoga mat on the floor, or lying on a bed.

So let's get started with the breathing exercises given below.

Deep Breathing

Follow the steps given below and relieve your stress within minutes.

1. *Take a few deep, nose-in breaths. Inhale deeply and relax.*

2. *Let your breath out of your nose.*

3. *Put a hand on your stomach. Keep your free hand on your heart.*

4. *Feel your stomach expand as you take a deep breath in. Feel your stomach drop as you exhale. It's preferable to shift your focus from your chest to your tummy.*

5. *Repeat this process three more times. Focus on filling your tummy with air as you inhale and exhale.*

Breathe Focus

This exercise is similar to deep breathing but allows you to use your imagination and think of a calming picture. Follow the steps given below:

1. *To help you unwind while you breathe deeply, try visualizing a peaceful scene and repeating a soothing word or phrase to yourself.*

2. *If your eyes are open, close them.*

3. *Breathe in deeply for a moment.*

4. *Inhale deeply. While doing it, picture a wave of tranquility washing over you. See if you can feel it all over your body.*

5. *Let out a sigh. Think of all your worries floating away with the air as you do it.*

6. *Now, while holding your breath, say a word or phrase. As you take a deep breath, tell yourself, "I inhale in harmony and calm."*

7. *Just as you let out a deep sigh, tell yourself, "I exhale out stress and pressure."*

8. *Keep going for another 10-20 minutes.*

Focusing on your Health and Diet

Women should pay special attention to their diet. Eating healthily throughout your life may curb cravings, maintain a healthy weight, increase your energy, become stress relieved and feel great. *Maintaining a nutritious diet may be challenging for any woman trying to juggle the needs of her loved ones, her career, and her education, not to mention the pressures of social media among teenage girls to present themselves in a particular manner, even via their food choices.* However, eating well may help you feel better emotionally, physically, and mentally as you progress through the many phases of a woman's life.

When you feel your stress levels rising, there are several things you can do to control them. Your relationship with food may be a powerful ally or enemy. What you eat may either help you relax or add to your frazzled state, so it's essential to be mindful of your eating habits if you're stressed. In addition, some nutrients, such as vitamins C and B, selenium, and magnesium, maybe more critical during stress.

Here are some foods that girls can include in their diet to keep them healthy, happy and powerful enough to enjoy their teenage years to the fullest.

Carbohydrates from whole grains

Some carbohydrates can have a calming effect. Serotonin is a hormone that helps raise mood and reduce stress, and carbs can increase serotonin levels. Increased levels of serotonin lead to more focused and efficient working. Selecting healthy carbohydrates, however, is essential. One study found that eating refined carbohydrates like chips, cookies, and crackers was associated with increased inflammation, stress, and sadness levels. Sweet potatoes and whole grains (including whole-grain bread, quinoa, brown rice, and oats) are good examples of foods that contain complex carbohydrates.

Bananas

Avoid Starbucks and grab a banana if you need a fast energy boost. The magnesium levels drop during stressful periods, but the bright, potassium-rich fruit includes the mood-boosting neurotransmitter dopamine. The B vitamins in bananas, particularly vitamin B6, support healthy nervous system function and are linked to reduced stress and improved energy levels.

Nuts

There are several ways in which eating nuts benefits your health. For one, they're filling and can prevent you from snacking unhealthily. Second, nuts may be able to assist in reducing blood pressure, and the Vitamin B present in them might help reduce anxiety. Nuts are high in calories, so don't consume more than a tiny handful at a time to avoid gaining weight.

Deep, Leafy Greens

Even though you think desk salads are dull, they might be one of the finest lunch options for relieving stress. Raw fruits and vegetables, incredibly dark leafy greens like spinach and kale, nuts and seeds have been shown to have a calming effect on the body and mind. Leafy greens, a good magnesium source, can reduce stress and blood pressure.

Fried Fish

Eating fatty fish can help strengthen your heart and improve your mood during stressful times. Omega-3 fatty acids, which may be found in whole fish like tuna, halibut, salmon, and sardines are suitable for your heart, and they may help alleviate sadness.

Practice Introspection

Take a minute to sit still and evaluate each of your emotions in silence. Note which emotions are more vital.

After this, ask yourself some questions and try answering them individually.

- *Ask yourself, "What do I feel?" rather than, "Why do I feel this way?" Be curious about your thoughts and emotions.*

- *Then, ask yourself if the thought is realistic.*

- *Later on, consider what happened in the past in similar situations and evaluate if your thoughts are on course with what happened.*

- *Actively challenge the thought and look for alternative explanations.*

- *Think of what you would gain versus lose by continuing to believe the thought.*

- *Consider what you would tell a friend having the same thought.*

Meditative Walking

Find an area without distractions, and you may stroll. There shouldn't be any noise or traffic, and the ground should be level enough that you won't trip. Once you've settled on a good spot, you may start each session by establishing your anchor. Relax and focus on your breathing while you pay close attention to your physical self for a moment. Feel the solidity of the floor beneath your feet, and after this, begin a gentle stroll. Instead of concentrating on your breathing when practicing walking meditation, you should pay close attention to your feet, legs, and the forward motion of your entire body.

It's as simple as taking a few calm, thoughtful laps around the block. Be as aware as possible of the movement of your feet and the sensations they evoke as you turn around or around a corner. You can always pause what you're doing, stretch, and assess how you're feeling. Take mental notes as you track the shifting bodily sensations during your stroll.

Just be yourself, stroll as usual, and have an open mind and heart. Walk for at least 10 minutes to experience a significant impact.

Aroma Therapy

In recent years, aromatherapy has become increasingly popular. Essential oils, candles, and other aromatherapy items have recently been popular because they may reduce stress, help calm anxious infants, and even improve overall health. Here are several practical applications of aromatherapy that teenage girls may use immediately.

Include it in your shower routine

Many individuals feel that a long, hot bath is the perfect remedy when under stress. Adding a few drops of essential oil to your bath water might help you unwind and enjoy the experience even more.

Light up an Aromatherapy Candle

Aromatherapy with candles is a beautiful option. Getting some aromatherapy candles and lighting them is one of the easiest methods to give a place a pleasant aroma and atmosphere. As with incense, the candles can provide a calming mood or be a focal point for prayer or meditation. However, because they produce less smoke, they might be more convenient than other types of incense.

Spray it on your clothes

Common uses for lavender include its ability to promote restful sleep and reduce anxiety. Spraying this essential oil onto your sheets and towels after diluting it with water could help you sleep better and reduce stress.

4 A's Stress Management Strategy

When you're under a lot of pressure, it might seem like carrying around a more prominent and heavier load as the day progresses.

The good news is that there are four strategies for lowering stress and adapting to the unavoidable pressures of daily life:

Avoidance

Some of the little pressures that bother individuals can be avoided by focusing on the tips below.

- Stop letting stress rule your day and start taking action to improve your circumstances. The purchase of a new CD, for instance, may transform a problematic trip into a pleasant one.

- Put some space between yourself and the source of your stress. If a class fellow constantly grates on your nerves, distance yourself from them.

Alteration

Get your point through and make your demands known. The impact can be enormous if you only follow these simple tips given below:

- Ask someone to stop maltreating you while maintaining your dignity. When expressing your emotions to another person, try using "I" phrases.

- Be upfront about your constraints. You may say, "I have only a few minutes for a conversation."

Acceptance

Acceptance may be a great stress reliever when denying or trying to change the situation. No matter how big the situation is, you can accept it by following the tips below.

- Share your feelings with someone you trust. Talk it through with a friend, family member, or therapist by giving them a call or setting up a coffee date.

- Just let it go and forgive. The ability to accept complex events and move on is crucial since worrying about things you can't change is counterproductive.

Adaptation

Changing how you evaluate and approach complex events might help you deal with them more effectively:

- Don't try to be ideal. Make substitutions in your daily life that are both reasonable and effective.

- Pick meals that will make dinnertime less stressful while satisfying everyone in the family.

- Stop going over distressing events in your brain.

Schedule out your stress.

In times of uncertainty, our top priorities always jump out at us. If we do, we save time on things that are high on someone else's list but not ours or that are simple but unimportant. It's easy to feel overwhelmed by all that needs to be done if our priorities aren't set. To prevent this from happening, we need to establish what tasks are most important and devote 95% of our time to them while saying "no" to everything else.

Keeping a Gratitude Journal

A positive and powerful technique to build emotional strength and decrease stress is to cultivate an attitude of appreciation for the people, things, and experiences in one's life.

You can do this by keeping a gratitude journal and expressing your feelings, thoughts, and emotions. Here are some journal prompts that will help you through your journey.

My Gratitude Journal Prompts

1. What are the things that made you happy today?

2. Describe something that you once had taken for granted but now appreciate.

3. What was your favorite part about this week?

4. What are the things that calm you down when you feel sad? How can you do those things more often in life?

5. When you review your friendships, who are the friends that make your life better?

6. What are the things that you like the most about yourself?

7. What friendships make you feel loved and appreciated?

8. What is your passion? Are you pursuing your passion?

9. What is your favorite season and why do you feel grateful for it?

10. What are the things that you look forward to in life?

Let's Solve These Worksheets Together

Here are a few worksheets you can solve to reduce stress and anxiety and lead a healthy and positive life.

My Not-To-Do List

Everything I should complete	Responsibilities of others
	Things I cannot control
	Stuff that exhausts me
	Stuff that can wait

My peaceful picture

Imagine your favorite place while closing your eyes. Now, imagine that you are here at this place and enjoying every detail of this place. Try to visualize everything that you can. Afterwards, draw all the things that you remember in the space given below.

My peaceful picture

You can also cut your drawing and paste it somewhere where you can view it every day. When anxiety or stress strikes you, just have a look at this picture and imagine you are back at your peaceful spot!

Fighting My Negative Thoughts

"By changing your thinking, you change your reality"

What are the things that upset me the most?

_____

_____

_____

What are the effects of my feelings on my behavior?

_____

_____

_____

What are some irrational ideas and beliefs I hold in a worrisome situation?

_____

_____

_____

How can I view this situation more positively?

_____

_____

_____

Chapter 3: Your Mind Must be Stronger than Your Feelings

Taking control over one's thoughts is the first step in developing self-discipline. If you can't keep your thoughts under control, you won't be able to keep your actions under control, either.

3.1: Our Mind Determines and Shapes Our Lives

You need to reach a point when other people's insignificant acts no longer affect how you feel. Don't let other people decide what you should do with your life. Don't let your feelings get the better of your brain.

Everyone is so busy these days that they forget to stop and appreciate the simple act of being alive. They are so tense about the future that they do not live in the moment.

What is mindfulness?

One definition of mindfulness is "intentional, nonjudgmental attention to the present moment." To be attentive is to observe one's internal experiences without attaching to them or passing judgment. That's because when we're conscious, we can look at things without letting our emotions cloud our judgment. When people cannot practice mindfulness, they frequently become mired in destructive patterns in which their thoughts provoke bad emotions, leading to harmful actions (such as substance abuse).

As with any other talent, mindfulness can be honed with time and effort. *Mindfulness isn't about forcing ourselves to think positively or suppress negative ideas; instead, it's the opposite: attentive individuals are aware of their emotions without condemning themselves for experiencing them. Mindfulness training strengthens our "mental muscles" and helps us separate our ideas from our actions.* Understanding the value of reflection over reflexive behavior is crucial.

Mindful VS Mind Full

We all like to be happy, but achieving it can be challenging when our thoughts never stop racing. This is when the distinction between mindful and mind full becomes clear.

To be mindful is to pay attention, stay in the present, and let things unfold without attaching any value or meaning to them. On the other side, having a mind-full approach indicates being preoccupied with one's thoughts, whether happy or sad, nostalgic or anxious.

Since most of the time, we let our brains run on autopilot; it's easy to get stuck in a loop of mind fullness. We miss out on the best parts of life because we are too busy rushing through it. When was the last time you stopped what you were doing and just lived? Do you focus on what you're reading, or do your mind wander to other things?

So, step back from the hectic pace of life and reflect on what you value most. Being alert and present at the moment is essential for appreciating life. These thoughtful moments are the essence of happiness. Mindfulness is the deliberate decision to focus on the now rather than ruminating over the past or planning for the future. Put life on hold for a while and think about what matters. Consider the things that mean the most to you, such as the time you spend with loved ones. Being alert and being present in the here and now allows us to savor every moment to its utmost.

3.2: The Moments You Focus on Prosper

What you give your attention to grows. If you want to make progress in your life, you need to start talking about the outcomes you desire rather than dwelling on the problems you're now facing.

Reasons behind not being mindful

Many go about their days mindlessly, the opposite of practicing mindfulness. We do things automatically, out of habit, and we make decisions and appraisals without paying much attention. At times, we lose touch with the world, our bodies and our brains. When we're in this state, our feelings appear to be happening to us rather than being something we can actively manage. Here are a few reasons to be more mindful and live in the present.

- *Distraction from the present results from dwelling on the past and the future*

- *Multitasking*

- *The state of denial*

- *Having an insistence on one's ideas or perceptions*

- *Blocking one's mind from considering anything*

- *Failing to make an effort*

- *Becoming emotionally coldhearted*

- *Having an opinion about anything, whether positive or negative*

Importance of Mindfulness in Your Personal Life

There are several mental and physiological gains from cultivating mindfulness. The following are some of the most significant health benefits:

• Positive Attitude and Mood

Being Mindful increases happiness and decreases stress and anxiety. Compared to antidepressant medicines, one research indicated that mindfulness training was just as beneficial in avoiding a relapse into depression.

- ## Stress Buster

The practice of mindfulness can mitigate stress and its effects. This helps in several ways for your health, including reducing blood pressure and boosting the immune system.

- ## Enhanced Immunity

Mindfulness meditation helps people with chronic pain cope better and feel less pain and emotional discomfort. Despite their discomfort, they are more active.

- ## Facilitates weight control

Mindfulness practices can help minimize binge eating and weight gain. It also helps people become mindful of their habits and control their desires.

- ## Overcome Insecure Relationships

Mindfulness training is an excellent tool for helping those struggling to form or maintain relationships. A person's desire for safety (relieving anxiety) overrides all other wants and emotions, making them more inclined to respond quickly or act out while feeling threatened. These people can benefit from practicing mindfulness because it teaches them to STOP, rest, observe, and then go on.

Training to Manage Your Feelings

Individuals who want to reap the benefits of mindfulness training should set aside quiet time first thing in the morning to sit, pay attention, and reflect. They'll be better able to respond to situations as they happen and enjoy life more by adopting this habit. Mindfulness may be practiced at any time during the day, including while the person is experiencing negative emotions like worry or anger. This technique provides a sense of serenity not contingent on any external cause.

Importance of Mindfulness in Your Academic Life

Mindfulness training has been demonstrated to improve teenagers' cognitive abilities, specifically their ability to use the brain's administrative processes. Examples of executive functions are the capacity to focus, shift attention, keep track of details, make plans, and recall information.

One research followed a class of 9th graders who participated in an eight-week mindfulness program at school. Compared to a control group, the students who participated in the study demonstrated considerable gains in self-control and concentration.

Training oneself in mindfulness can help one focus and pay more attention. With regular practice, your memory could improve, and your brain power could soar.

Another study discovered that high school students who participated in a four-week mindfulness program outperformed their peers in attention-based activities. They also fared higher on standardized assessments of learning and development. They also improved more in areas that are indicators of academic achievement in the future.

3.3: The Secret to Success in Life is Resilience and Positive Mental Health

As with any other talent, mindfulness can be honed with time and effort. Mindfulness isn't about forcing ourselves to think positively or rein in our negative emotions; instead, it's the opposite: aware individuals accept their feelings without criticizing themselves for experiencing them.

What is meant by Resilience?

The capacity to deal with adversity and bounce back from it is called resilience. Those who can maintain composure in the face of adversity are resilient. The ability to pull together one's resources, seek assistance when required, and discover solutions to one's problems are hallmarks of a resilient individual. Those who are mentally tough can draw on their resources to overcome obstacles such as those associated with:

- *Loss of a family member*

- *Breakups*

- *Concerns about money*

- *A medical condition*

- *Reduced employment*

- *Urgent healthcare needs*

- *Academic Stresses*

Importance of Resilience

Having Resilience allows people to mentally and emotionally handle storms of adversity. Inner toughness allows individuals to manage difficult situations without completely crumbling. According to psychologists, resilient people can pick themselves up after a setback and continue living fulfilling lives. It is a fact of life that we will all experience loss and change. Everybody has some difficulty in life at some point. Not getting into a class or being passed over in your school's play audition examples of relatively modest obstacles, whereas natural disasters like storms and terrorist attacks are far more severe.

Those who aren't resilient may crack under pressure. They may have difficulty moving on from negative thoughts and resort to unhealthy coping techniques. According to psychology, how people respond to such challenges can have profound effects, both in the short and long term.

Stress and hardships in life will still be there even if you develop resilience. Those who have this trait don't paint a rosy picture of reality for themselves. They have internalized the reality that life may sometimes be frustrating and challenging. They still feel the pain of loss but can better get past it and rebuild their lives because of their positive approach.

The Link between Mindfulness and Resilience

Mindfulness entails paying attention to and actively participating in the here and now. The ability to swiftly get over setbacks, in general, is one definition of resilience. **Though some people appear to be born with greater resilience than others, this quality may still be taught. One of the best ways to strengthen resilience is through mindfulness.** Mindfulness training is far more effective than relaxation training in bolstering resilience.

Moreover, compared to those who got relaxation training, those who received mindfulness training were more inclined to continue and practice independently. This standard bolsters sound effects and long-term resilience. Mindfulness and obsessive, racing thoughts have been found to have a detrimental correlation with ruminating. If we are more self-aware, we are less prone to get mired in a cycle of obsessive thinking.

What is Positive Mental health?

A condition of good mental health is one in which an individual can:

- *Live up to his or her abilities*
- *Work well*
- *Manage life's normal challenges*
- *Give back to one's society*

One's sense of self, one's resiliency in the face of adversity, and the caliber of one's interpersonal connections all contribute to one's mental and psychological health.

Remember that being in good mental health is more than just not suffering from mental health problems. Positive traits like a sense of purpose, satisfaction, sustaining good relationships, and active participation in life are at the heart of what it means to be mentally healthy.

The Importance of a Positive Mental Health

When people are in a condition of positive mental health, they are emotionally and behaviorally healthy and strong. Optimal mental health is linked to fewer instances of clinical depression and long-term health problems. If people take steps to enhance their mental health, they can "get forward of the trend" and avoid depression in the first place.

Scientists have shown that when individuals are pleased, they are more open to new information. Optimists are more receptive to new opportunities and relationships. One's optimism and sense of well-being are directly related to their resilience in the face of adversity.

The Link between Mindfulness and Positive Mental Health

Being mindful tends to improve physical and mental health. Studies based on mindfulness by therapists have shown that it decreases anxiety and depression. Mindfulness has also been shown to reduce blood pressure and increase sleep quality. This method may aid in the reduction of discomfort. There are two possible mechanisms via which mindfulness aids depression. *The first benefit is that it trains you to live here and now. And second, practicing mindfulness can help you "de-center" those ideas.* Just like sitting on the bank of a river and watching the leaves drift by, one may do the same with one's thoughts. By training your attention to remain present in the now, you may avoid getting swept away by fleeting thoughts. Ideas like "it's constantly going to be the same" or "none of it ever goes to benefit me" are common depressants. *You may learn to detach yourself from these harmful mental patterns with time and effort using mindfulness and gain a positive outlook on your life.*

3.4: The Whole Universe Bows Down to a Still Mind

You must rely on your five senses to keep cool in a challenging and demanding situation. Sitting still and chugging water won't help you relax. You may do numerous things to calm yourself and restore your wits, but keep in mind that it may take some time.

Here are some ways to practice mindfulness and bring more peace into your life:

• The Body Scanning Exercise

The Body Scanning Exercise is simple to start with and doesn't require special equipment or props.

To do this exercise, you have to take a deep breath with your nose and let it out through your lips while relaxing in a comfortable chair. As you let out your breath, close your eyes. Take note of your current physical sensations. Begin with the crown of the head and work your way down, pausing to note how different parts of your body feel. Remember that you're not attempting to alter anything; instead, you're simply tuning into how your entire body feels as you systematically examine it from head to toe.

• The Candle Exercise

The Candle Exercise entails staring fixedly at a candle for several minutes. Focus, mental health, sleep, and spiritual health may all benefit from candle gazing meditation. However, this has to be confirmed by further study.

Carry out this exercise by following the steps given below.

- *Relax and make yourself at home. Relax your eyes and focus on the target of your attention.*

- *You can either stare at the flame without blinking and risk having your eyes moist and tear up, or you may alternate between the two. Close your eyes if you like, and think about the positive energy and purpose you wish to bring into the room.*

- *You may like to practice grounding, to send love and compassion, to sense the gentle hum of inspiration and the sweet whisper of thanks in the light, or some combination of these. It's lovely and fitting, no matter what you have in mind.*

- *Take a break and relax in your quiet, holy spot.*

- *Cup your hands about your eyes and shut them when you're ready. You may close your eyes and look into the darkness created by your clasped hands instead. Relax and massage your own body.*

- *Thank yourself for trying to tap into your inner and outer sources of enlightenment. If you have a lighted candle, please thank it and blow it out. You've had enough practice for now.*

• Initiate Mantras

Teenage females, in particular, might benefit from mantras since many feel pressured to conform to societal norms or gain popularity. *Affirmations may assist in shifting someone's mentality and give them strength by reminding them of their distinct qualities when they feel like changing for other people's love and acceptance.*

Here are some mantras you can practice daily and feel a change in your life immediately.

My Mantras for a Happier Me!

I have all the space to learn new things and grow.

I am just who I am and I love it.

My inner wisdom is reliable, thus I pay attention to it and follow it.

For the most part, I let my feelings do what they're supposed to.

I treat myself with all the kindness and love that I deserve.

My passion and intentions help me succeed.

Single Tasking

In contrast to multitasking, single-tasking means giving undivided attention to and completing a single task before going on to another. Though more difficult to create and maintain, it yields more significant productivity gains.

When you single-task, you give full attention to a single activity while minimizing interruptions. The plan is to finish what you're working on or accomplish some predetermined objective before moving on to anything else.

Here are some simple tips for practicing single-tasking.

1. Organize

Clutter makes it difficult to concentrate on a single task. A continual distraction is created by clutter, whether in your living space, workplace, or even desk. Take time to sanitize everything around you before beginning your journey toward single-tasking.

2. Identify what's most important to you.

The question to ask oneself is, "What is the single most significant task I have to complete now?" Create a list of everything you need to get done today, and then pare it down to no more than five items. When you're done making your list, prioritize the items by placing numbers from 1 to 5 next. Then you may proceed with each assignment. Always get one job done before starting on another.

3. Try to do it every day.

You could find yourself reverting to your old multitasking habits despite trying to avoid doing so. Like with meditation, regular practice brings comfort.

Mindful Eating

A "Mindful Eating" practice encourages diners to take their time and savor each bite. Although it may sound obvious, it is common for our brains to be preoccupied with addressing problems at mealtime.

The following are some commonplace tips for implementing a mindful eating routine:

- *When you eat, you focus solely on eating.*

- *Get your senses involved.*

- *Pay attention to your senses when you eat.*

- *Keep an eye on your thoughts and gently bring them back to the here and now whenever they wander.*

- *Be kind to yourself and use patience.*

- *Pay attention to how you feel in your body.*

- *Think about where your food comes from.*

- *Notice how different foods make you feel.*

- *Create a positive perspective on eating.*

Mindful Gardening

The garden setting is perfect for practicing mindfulness since we can fully immerse ourselves in the sensory experience of planting seeds, trimming shrubs, or weeding a garden. The garden is ideal for tuning out distractions and focusing on the present.

The first step toward more mindful gardening is using all five senses. Here are a few questions to think about while doing mindful gardening.

Hearing: *How can I use my hearing to be more present at the moment?*

Touch: *How might I utilize my sense of touch to focus right now?*

Smell: *How can I become immersed in the here and now using the power of smell?*

Sight: *How can I utilize my eyes to immerse myself in this very moment?*

Taste: *How can I become more present using my sense of taste at this time?*

Music Therapy

Listening to music is a form of musical mindfulness exercise. Lyrics, beats, pauses, and individual instruments may all be monitored. If you listen this way, you'll be more in tune with the music and present now. Keeping a music journal is a great way to keep track of your emotions and ideas. As you listen to the music, you get more in tune with what's happening for you right now.

Let's solve these worksheets together.

Here are a few simple worksheets for you to solve to grasp more grip on mindfulness and living a healthy and happy life.

Self-Reflection on My Happiness

Who did you decide to be today?

_____

_____

_____

_____

Describe in 4 words the person you look up to:

_____

_____

_____

_____

You become the happiest when...

You become unhappy when...

3 Things that are mood boosters for me

1 Someone that inspires and motivates me

2 Things that amuse me

Enhancing Greatness

Name: _____

How do you want to feel today?

_____

_____

_____

_____

_____

How can you make your day better for yourself?

_____

_____

_____

How can you make others feel happy because of you?

_____

_____

_____

Your greatest win of the day is...

_____

_____

_____

Things that you can enhance

_____

_____

_____

My Instant Mindful Therapy

How do I feel right now?

What are the current thoughts in my mind at the moment?

_____

_____

_____

_____

How does my body feel right now?

_____

_____

_____

_____

_____

_____

_____

Breathe

Start deep breathing while inhaling through your nose and exhaling the air through your mouth. Exhale longer than inhale and try to expand your belly while inhaling. Do this activity for 5 minutes and see the difference yourself!

A Goodbye Letter

Tell yourself that it's okay to feel. Let your inner light shine brightly. Don't be frightened to heal; love within you. If you feel like the ocean sometimes, let it roar. Don't be frightened to speak up against the stillness within you.

If you want to change the world, you must first change yourself. Time may fly by, and you'll look back and wonder why you didn't take more time for yourself during your life. You must remember that putting effort into bettering yourself is the finest investment. Thus begin today's date with self-care. Release all your self-doubts and fears and start today to become the most positive and healthy version of yourself!

No one can reject opposing emotions like love and hatred, joy and sorrow, fury and calm, or exhaustion and repose; similarly, no one can deny the existence of fate that is sometimes beyond our control. That is not to say that you will be dominated by it. You know in your heart that there are things you need to say. Quit holding everyone else responsible for your misfortunes. Accept responsibility for the times when you could have said "no" but didn't, for the times when you could have spoken out but instead covered your mouth. Accept the consequences of your restraints and the decisions you may have taken. Forgive yourself and promise to start working on yourself to become better.

Be deliberate in all that you do. There's no need to feel guilty about wanting to concentrate. It would help if you took pride in that. You won't have to go out of your way to seize chances if you have a firm grasp of your current role and a detailed plan for your future. Possibilities will come to you. In time, joy will find you. And instead of having options presented to you, you will be the one making the call.

Conclusion

As you come to the end of this book, I know you are feeling a new light in yourself, you are feeling a new strength and power inside of you. You are no longer afraid of things not going in your direction because you know that you are strong enough to handle them.

You are no longer tensed up about the words of others because you have come to realize your own worth and true self. You have forgiven yourself for the times when you thought you were never good enough or for the times when you compared yourself to the other pretty girls. You have a vision for yourself, you have goals to chase and dreams to fulfill now.

You are no longer stressed about your grades, your appearance, and the disagreements in your family or even going out with your friends. You feel confident enough to overcome anything that scares you or tenses you up.

Hopefully, your journey with "Wisdom Workbook for Teenage Girls 13-18" has enhanced not only your self-esteem, but has also improved your cognitive, logical and emotional well-being. I am hopeful that now you will start your day with a positive and energetic side of you and at the end of the day, have all of your tasks completed.

You know the importance of living in the moment and the benefits of practicing mindfulness. These practices would improve your relationships, and your academic life and would also improve your ability to tackle and bounce back from difficult situations. You can now finally start to live a healthy, fulfilling and positive life!

Looking forward to seeing a better and strong you.

THANK YOU

Printed in Great Britain
by Amazon

37479405R00044